不要哭，狡猾！
Don't Cry, Sly!

retold by
Henriette Barkow

illustrated by
Richard Johnson

Chinese translation
by Sylvia Denham

mantra

「刷牙啊！梳理頭髮啊！」
不論狡猾怎樣做，他的媽媽
總是不滿的。

狡猾的媽媽時常都大聲叫喊。
「收拾你的房間啊！洗碗碟啊！」

"Brush your teeth! Comb your hair!"
And however much Sly did, it was
never enough for his mum.

Sly's mum was always shouting:
"Tidy your room! Do the dishes!"

隔壁的小紅雞可以聽得很清楚，她不喜歡
狡猾的媽媽不停的叫喊聲。

Next door Little Red could hear everything. She hated the way Sly's mum
always screamed and shouted.

有一天，她聽到大叫的聲音：
「我想吃燒雞啊！」
小紅雞覺得非常害怕。

One day she heard a scream:
"I want roast chicken!"
And Little Red became very
very scared.

狡猾也很害怕，他從未捉過一隻雞，但他是一隻聰明的狐狸，他已經有一個計劃了。

Sly was scared too, he'd never caught a hen before, but being a smart fox he had a plan.

當小紅雞出外時，狡猾偷偷走進她的
屋裏，一直等到她回來。

When Little Red went out Sly sneaked into her house and waited
and waited, until she returned.

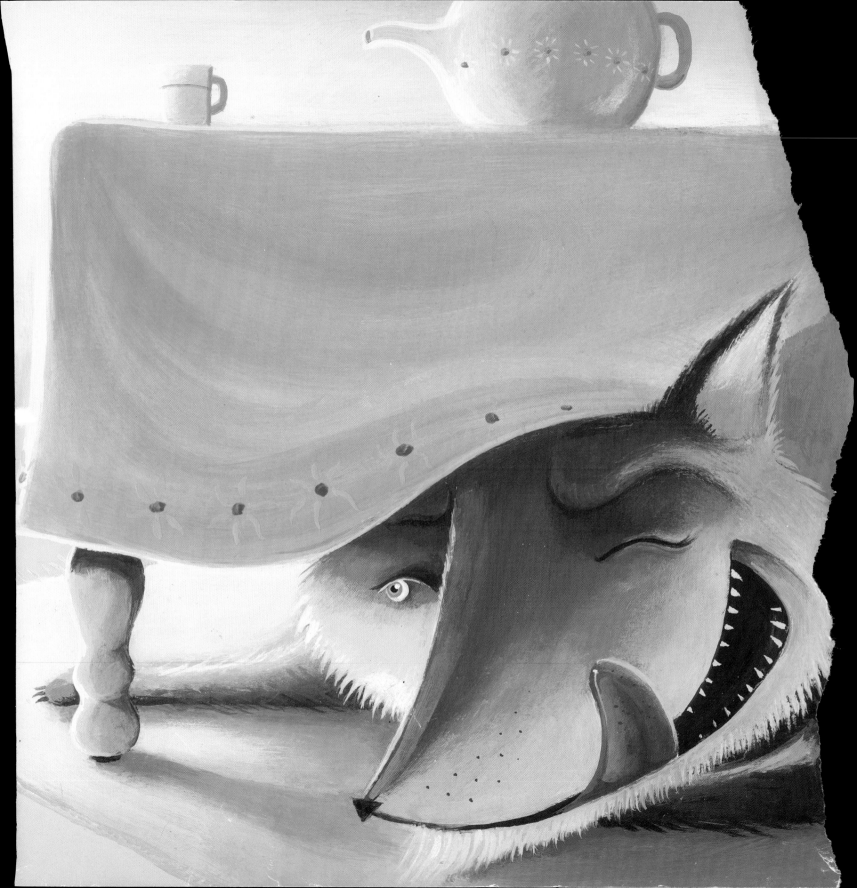

「救命呀！救命呀！」當她見到
狡猾時，小紅雞一邊叫，
一邊跳到書架上面去，
但這對狡猾絕不成問題，畢竟他是
一隻有計劃的狐狸。

"Help! Help!" Little Red cried when
she saw Sly and jumped up onto the
top of the bookcase.
But that was no problem for Sly, after
all, he was a fox with a plan.

狡猾開始追著自己的尾巴團團轉，
越轉越快，直至…

Sly started spinning round and round, chasing his tail.
Faster and faster he went until...

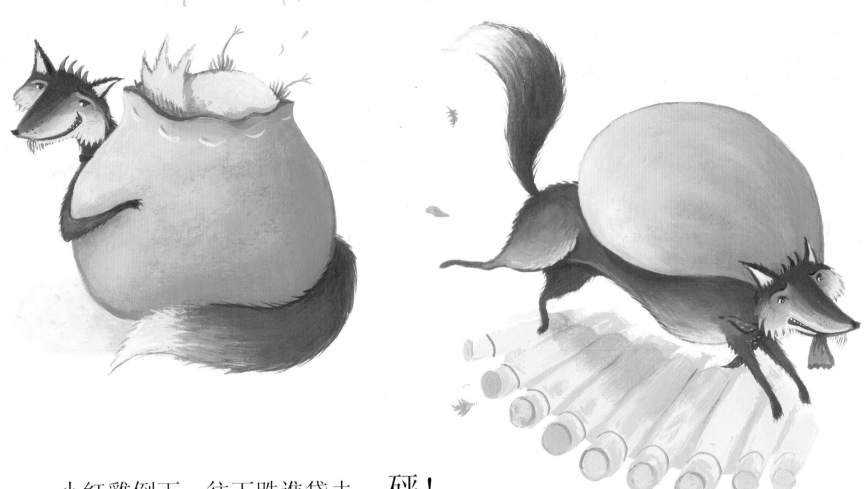

…小紅雞倒下，往下跌進袋去 - 砰！

狡猾將袋子拖下樓梯 - 砰咚！ 砰咚！ 砰！

…Little Red fell down, down, down into the sack - THUMP!

Sly dragged the sack down the stairs - THUMPADY, THUMPADY, BUMP!

當他抵達地下時，他已經又累又頭暈眼花，
就在樓梯下睡著了。

By the time he reached the ground he was
so tired and dizzy that he fell asleep at the
bottom of the stairs.

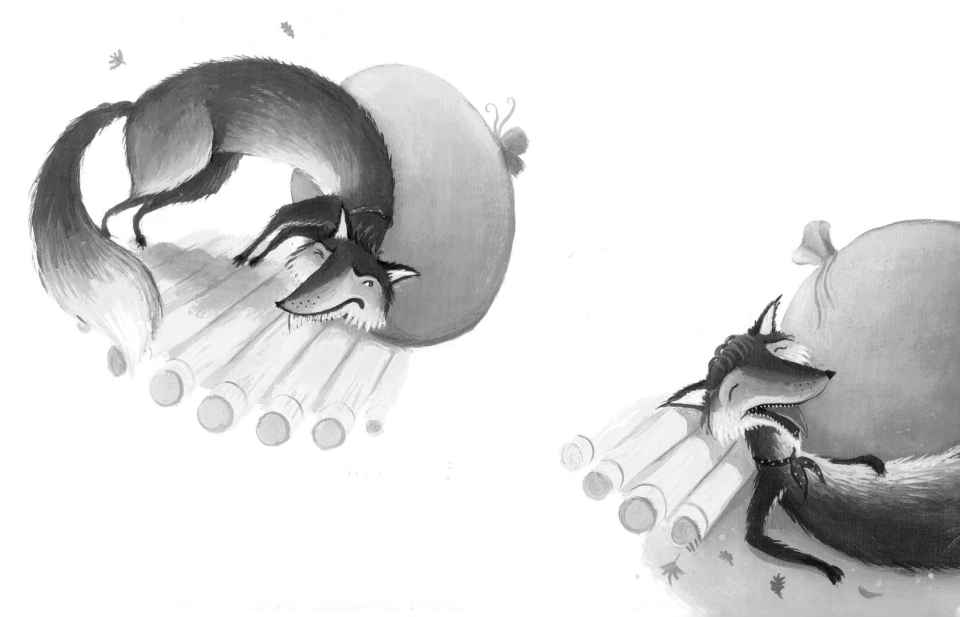

Now was Little Red's chance.

這是小紅雞的機會了，

她擠身出袋子外，盡速跑上樓梯。

She squeezed herself out of the sack and ran as
fast as she could, up, up, up the stairs.

當小紅雞恢復元氣時，她想到可憐的狡猾和他
即將要面對的麻煩，她可以怎樣幫他呢？

When Little Red had recovered she thought about poor Sly and all the trouble
he would be in. What could she do to help?

她看看廚房周圍，終於想出一個辦法。

She looked around her kitchen and then she had an idea.

當她做完後，她叫醒狡猾，並將她的計劃告訴他。

When she had finished she woke Sly and told him of her plan.

狡猾拿著沉重的袋子回家。
他弄好晚餐，擺好飯桌，
然後叫他的媽媽：
「燒雞已準備好，快來吃呀！」

Sly went home with his heavy sack.
He made the dinner and set the
table, and then he called his mum.
"Roast chicken is ready, come and
get it!"

狻猊的媽媽有沒有大叫大喊呢？
她高興得大叫，歡呼的喊著說：
「這是我吃過的晚餐中最好的一餐啊！」

And did Sly's mum scream and shout?
She screamed with delight.
She shouted with joy: "That's the best
dinner I've ever had!"

由那天開始，狡猾負責所有的煮飯和做菜，他有一位新朋友幫他，
而他的媽媽也只是偶然嘮叨責罵他。

From that day forth Sly did all the cooking with the help of his new friend.
And Sly's mum, well she only nagged him now and then.

To the children of Mrs Michelsen's Class of 02
at Moss Hall Junior School
H.B.

For my friends, Rebecca Edwards
and Richard Holland
R.J.

Mantra
5 Alexandra Grove, London N12 8NU
www.mantralingua.com